U.S. Fish & Wildlife Service

Revised Comprehensive Conservation Plan and Environmental Impact Statement

Alaska Peninsula and Becharof National Wildlife Refuges

U.S. Fish and Wildlife Service Mission Statement

The mission of the U.S. Fish and Wildlife Service is working with others to conserve, protect, and enhance fish, wildlife, plants, and their habitats for the continuing benefit of the American people.

Refuge Mission Statement

The mission of the National Wildlife Refuge System is to administer a national network of lands and waters for the conservation, management, and, where appropriate, restoration of the fish, wildlife, and plant resources and their habitats within the United States for the benefit of present and future generations of Americans.

—National Wildlife Refuge System Improvement Act of 1997

The comprehensive conservation plan details program planning levels that are substantially greater than current budget allocations and, as such, is for strategic planning and program prioritization purposes only. This plan does not constitute a commitment for staffing increases or funding for future refuge-specific land acquisitions, construction projects, or operational and maintenance increases.

Revised Comprehensive Conservation Plan and Environmental Impact Statement

Alaska Peninsula and Becharof National Wildlife Refuges

October 2005

Prepared by
U.S. Fish & Wildlife Service
Region 7
Anchorage, Alaska

Alaska Peninsula and Becharof
National Wildlife Refuges
P.O. Box 277
King Salmon, AK 99613

U.S. Fish & Wildlife Service
Region 7
1011 East Tudor Road
Anchorage, AK 99503

United States Department of the Interior

FISH AND WILDLIFE SERVICE
1011 East Tudor Rd.
Anchorage, Alaska 99503-6199

Dear Reader:

This Revised Comprehensive Conservation Plan (Plan) and Environmental Impact Statement (EIS) will guide management of the Alaska Peninsula and Becharof National Wildlife Refuges for the next 15 years. This Plan outlines four management alternatives, including the U.S. Fish & Wildlife Service's preferred alternative, and presents the Service's evaluation of the environmental consequences of each of those alternatives.

To develop this Plan, we analyzed and considered the almost 11,600 comments received on the Draft Plan, which was released in February 2004.

The Plan provides management direction for activities and uses of the Refuges, goals and objectives for the Refuges programs, and compatibility determinations for the current uses of the Refuges. The major change between the Draft Plan and this final Plan is that we developed a fourth alternative (3a) as the new preferred alternative. This alternative differs from the Draft plan preferred alternative in that it would require the refuge manager to consider applications for helicopter access on a case-by-case basis.

We will publish a Record of Decision 30 days after release of this final Plan. The Record of Decision will present the rational for selecting the course of action that will be followed by the Refuges.

You may also view the plan online at http://www.r7.fws.gov/nwr/planning/plans.htm.

Comments and requests for additional CD-ROMs or further information should be directed to

Peter Wikoff, Planning Team Leader
U.S. Fish & Wildlife Service
1011 East Tudor Rd, MS-231
Anchorage, AK 99503
fw7_APB_planning@fws.gov
(907) 786-3837

We thank everyone who participated in the planning and public involvement process.

Your comments helped us prepare a better plan for the future of this refuge.

Contents

Tables

Figures

Abbreviations and Acronyms

AAC	Alaska Administrative Code
ACMP	Alaska Coastal Management Program
ADF&G	Alaska Department of Fish and Game
AHRS	Alaska Heritage Resource Survey
ANCSA	Alaska Native Claims Settlement Act
ANHA	Alaska Natural History Association
ANILCA	Alaska National Interest Lands Conservation Act
ANSI	American National Standards Institute
ATV	all-terrain vehicle
BIA	Bureau of Indian Affairs
BLM	U.S. Bureau of Land Management
CE	categorical exclusion
CFR	Code of Federal Regulations
cfs	cubic feet per second
cfs/mi^2	cubic feet per second per square mile
CRSA	coastal resources service area
DLP	defense of life or property
DNR	Alaska Department of Natural Resources
EA	environmental assessment
EIS	environmental impact statement
EPA	Environmental Protection Agency
FAA	Federal Aviation Administration
fps	feet per second
FRWR	Federal Reserved Water Rights
GIS	geographic information systems
GMU	game management unit
I&M	inventory and monitoring
IACUC	Institutional Animal Care and Use Committee
KSVC	King Salmon Visitor Center
LCP	land conservation plan
LPP	land protection plan
MAPS	Monitoring Avian Productivity and Survivorship
mg/L	milligrams per liter
NAPCH	Northern Alaska Peninsula caribou herd
NEPA	National Environmental Policy Act
NWR	national wildlife refuge
ORV	off-road vehicle
PUMP	public-use management plan
RAWS	Remote Area Weather Stations
RONS	Refuge Operational Needs System

Service	U.S. Fish & Wildlife Service
System	National Wildlife Refuge System
TEA-21	Transportation Equity Act for the 21st Century
TUS	transportation and utility system
USGS	U.S. Geological Survey

Glossary

air transporter	An air taxi operator licensed by the Federal Aviation Administration who flies people to/from and/or within the Refuges. Transporters must have special-use permits to operate on the refuge.
allowed	Activity, use, or facility is allowed under existing National Environmental Policy Act (NEPA) analysis, a specific compatibility determination, and compliance with all applicable laws and regulations of the Service, other Federal agencies, and the State of Alaska.
not allowed	Activity, use, or facility is not allowed.
alternatives	Different ways to resolve issues, achieve refuge purposes, meet refuge goals, and contribute to the National Wildlife Refuge System mission. Alternatives provide different options to respond to major issues identified during the planning process.
"No Action Alternative"	The current management direction. With this alternative, no change from the current comprehensive conservation plan would be implemented.
"Preferred Alternative"	A proposed action in the NEPA document for the comprehensive conservation plan identifying the alternative that the Service believes best achieves planning unit purposes, vision, and goals; helps fulfill the Refuge System mission; maintains and, where appropriate, restores the ecological integrity of each refuge and the Refuge System; addresses the significant issues and mandates; and is consistent with principles of sound fish and wildlife management.
angler hour	One person fishing for one hour with recreational fishing gear (e.g., rod and reel).
archaeological resource	Any material remains of past human life or activities that are of archaeological interest. Materials that are capable of providing understanding of past human behavior, cultural adaptation, and related topics through the application of scholarly or scientific techniques.
authorized	Activity, use, or facility allowed upon issuance of a special-use permit or other authorization.

big-game guide outfit	Means to provide, for compensation or with the intent or with an agreement to receive compensation, big-game commercial hunting services in the field; a guide outfit includes accompanying or being present with a big-game hunter in the field, either personally or through an assistant; guide-outfit does not include the provision of transportation to, from, or in the field if the person providing the transportation and the person being transported do not stalk, pursue, track, kill or attempt to kill big game during the provision of transportation.
big-game guide	A big-game guide-outfitter is a person who has special-use permit to guide on a refuge and is licensed by the State of Alaska to provide services, equipment, or facilities to a big-game hunter in the field. A big-game guide accompanies or is present with, personally or through an assistant, the hunter in the field.
big-game outfitter	A big-game outfitter is a person who has special-use permit to provide services on the refuge and who provides services, supplies, or facilities to a big-game hunter in the field but does not accompany nor is present with the hunter in the field.
biological diversity	The variety of life, including the variety of living organisms, the genetic differences among them, and the communities in which they occur (USFWS, 602 FW 1.6).
biological integrity	Biotic composition, structure, and functioning at the genetic, organism, and community levels consistent with natural conditions, including the natural biological processes that shape genomes, organisms, and communities (USFWS, 602 FW 1.6).
campsite hardening	Actions undertaken to increase the durability of a campsite through manipulation such as placing gravel on a place to pitch a tent or trails within the campsite. Does not include facilities such as outhouses, picnic tables, etc., normally associated with campgrounds.
categorical exclusion (CE, CX, CATEX, CATX)	A category of actions that do not individually or cumulatively have a significant effect on the human environment and have been found to have no such effect in procedures adopted by a Federal agency pursuant to the National Environmental Policy Act (40 CFR 1508.4).
commercial recreational use	Recreational use of lands, waters, and resources for business or financial gain; includes guided recreational fishing, guided recreational hunting, other guided recreation, and air-taxi services.

compatible use	A proposed or existing wildlife-dependent recreational use or any other use of a refuge that, based on sound professional judgment, will not materially interfere with or detract from the fulfillment of the mission of the System or the purposes of the refuge (USFWS, 603 FW 2 2.6).
compatibility determination	A written determination signed and dated by the refuge manager and the Service regional chief signifying that a proposed or existing use of a national wildlife refuge is a compatible use or is not a compatible use. The director of the Service makes this delegation through the regional director (USFWS, 603 FW 2 2.6).
comprehensive conservation plan	A document that describes the desired future conditions of a refuge or planning unit and provides long-range guidance and management direction to achieve the purposes of the refuge; to help fulfill the mission of the Refuge System; to maintain and, where appropriate, restore the ecological integrity of each refuge and the Refuge System; to help achieve the goals of the National Wilderness Preservation System; and to meet other mandates. (USFWS, 602 FW 1.6).
cultural resources	Fragile nonrenewable properties, including any district, site, building, structure, or object significant in American history, architecture, archaeology, engineering, or culture. These resources are significant for information they contain or the associations they have with past people, events, or life ways (USFWS 1992).
ecological integrity	The integration of biological integrity, natural biological diversity, and environmental health; the replication of natural conditions (USFWS, 602 FW 1.6).
ecosystem	A biological community functioning together with its environment as a unit.
effects (wildlife and habitat)	
long-term effects	Effects occurring after or lasting longer than 5 years after implementation of the action.
major effects	Affecting a regional or local population of a species, or its habitat, sufficiently to cause a change in abundance or a change in distribution beyond which natural recruitment is not likely to return the population to its former abundance within several generations.
minor effects	Affecting the survival, reproduction, distribution, or behavior of a specific group of individuals of a population in a localized area for one generation or less without affecting the regional population. Habitat composition and structure remain

unchanged; habitat quality, however, may be affected by indirect actions (e.g., disturbance or displacement affecting a specific group of individuals that may result in altered use of an area).

moderate effects   Affecting a local population, or habitat quality and composition in a localized area, sufficiently to cause a change in abundance or distribution for more than one generation, but unlikely to affect the integrity of the regional population over the long term.

negligible effects   Temporary effects that do not result in a change in the survival, reproduction, distribution, or behavior of individuals. The ability of the habitat to support populations would remain unchanged (e.g., temporary disturbance of a specific group of individuals that does not result in a change in use of an area).

short-term effects   Effects that are anticipated to occur within five years from implementation of the action.

environmental assessment   A concise public document that provides a sufficient analysis for determining whether to prepare an environmental impact statement (EIS) or a finding of no significant impact. It also aids an agency's compliance with NEPA when no EIS is necessary (40 CFR 1508.9).

environmental health   Abiotic composition, structure, and functioning of the environment consistent with natural conditions, including the natural abiotic processes that shape the environment (USFWS, 602 FW 1.6).

environmental impact statement   A detailed written statement, required by section 102(2)(C) of the National Environmental Policy Act (NEPA), analyzing the environmental impacts of a proposed action, adverse effects of the project that cannot be avoided, alternative courses of action, short-term uses of the environment versus the maintenance and enhancement of long-term productivity, and any irreversible and irretrievable commitment of resources (40 CFR 1508.11).

floating facilities   Floathomes, floatcamps, floating lodges, floating caretaker facilities (including mariculture), floating recreational facilities, and other floating residential or commercial facilities located on shorelands, tidelands, or submerged lands.

goal   A descriptive, open-ended, and often broad statement of desired future conditions that conveys purposes but does not define measurable units (USFWS, 620 FW 1.6).

haul-out   A beach or other terrestrial coastal location used by marine mammals on a regular basis.

helicopter use for recreational access	Use of helicopters for other than official government management activities, search and rescue, or other authorized activities.
human food-conditioning	A behavior learned when an animal receives food, fish, or garbage from people.
human habituation	Decrease in natural responsiveness upon repeated exposure to a nonthreathening, human stimulus.
issue	Any unsettled matter that requires a management decision (e.g., a Service initiative, opportunity, resource management problem, a threat to the resources of the unit, conflict in uses, public concern, or the presence of an undesirable resource condition) (USFWS, 602 FW 1.6).
land use permit	An authorization issued by the State of Alaska for use of state land. Permits are issued by the Alaska Department of Natural Resources, Division of Mining, Land, and Water.
likelihood	
low	Effects are typically not expected, but could occur under unusual conditions.
medium	Effects are not expected to occur in the majority of instances.
high	Effects are anticipated to occur as a result of implementing the action.
marine transporter	A vessel operator, licensed by the U.S. Coast Guard, who provides water transportation services for people.
minimum-impact camping	Camping leaving little or no trace of human occupation. Techniques vary widely but include the following: selecting durable sites (such as gravel bars), proper disposal of human waste, packing out all litter not completely burned, having small fires or no fires (using stoves for cooking), leaving vegetation intact, removing evidence of campfires, using equipment and clothing that blend in with the setting, and being quiet.
national wildlife refuge	A designated area of land, water, or an interest in land or water within the National Wildlife Refuge System; does not include coordination areas. Find a complete listing of all units of the Refuge System in the current Annual Report of Lands Under Control of the U.S. Fish and Wildlife Service (USFWS 2003).

native species
A species, subspecies, or distinct population that occurs within its natural range or natural zone of potential dispersal (i.e., the geographic area the species occupies naturally or would occupy in the absence of direct or indirect human activity or an environmental catastrophe). This definition recognizes that ecosystems and natural ranges are not static; they can and do evolve over time. Thus a species may naturally extend its range onto (or within) a refuge and still be considered native.

navigable waters
Under Federal law, for the purpose of determining ownership of submerged lands beneath inland water bodies not reserved at the date of statehood, navigable waters are waters used or susceptible to being used in their ordinary condition as highways of commerce over which trade and travel are or may be conducted in the customary modes of trade and travel on water. In situations where navigability and the ownership of submerged lands are disputed, the final authority for determining navigability rests with the Federal courts.

National Environmental Policy Act (NEPA)
This act, promulgated in 1969, requires all Federal agencies to disclose the environmental effects of their actions, incorporate environmental information, and use public participation in the planning and implementation of all actions. Federal agencies must integrate NEPA with other planning requirements and must prepare appropriate NEPA documents to facilitate better environmental decision-making (from 40 CFR 1500). The law also established the Council on Environmental Quality to implement the law and to monitor compliance with the law.

nonconsumptive uses
Recreational activities (e.g., hiking, photography, and wildlife observation) that do not involve the taking or catching of fish, wildlife, or other natural resources.

noncommercial recreational uses
Recreational uses of lands, waters, and resources not for business or financial gain—including recreational fishing and hunting, floating, camping, hiking, photography, and sightseeing.

nonnative species
A species, subspecies, or distinct population that has been introduced by humans (intentionally or unintentionally) outside its natural range or natural zone of potential dispersal.

objective
A concise statement of what we want to achieve, how much we want to achieve, when and where we want to achieve it, and who is responsible for the work. Objectives derive from goals and provide the basis for determining strategies, monitoring refuge accomplishments, and evaluating the success of strategies. Objectives should be attainable, time-specific, and measurable (USFWS, 602 FW 1.6).

ordinary high water mark	The line on the shore established by the fluctuations of water and indicated by physical characteristics such as a clear, natural line impressed on the bank, shelving, changes in the character of soil, destruction of terrestrial vegetation, the presence of litter and debris, or other appropriate means that consider the characteristics of the surrounding area (33 CFR 328.3[e]).
permanent base camp	A camp with permanent or semipermanent structures that serves as a base of operations for recreational fishing, hunting, research, or other uses. In general, permanent base camps are larger and provide more comfort and amenities than do temporary base camps. The facilities cannot be readily dismantled or moved and normally remain in place from year to year.
primitive tent camps	Portable camps, normally consisting of small tents, used by nonguided and guided visitors. They usually remain in place when in use and then are disassembled and removed.
public	Individuals, organizations, and groups; officials of Federal, state, and local government agencies; Indian tribes; Native organizations; and foreign nations. Public may include anyone outside the core planning team. It includes those who may or may not have indicated an interest in Service issues and those who do or do not realize that Service decisions may affect them.
public involvement	A process that offers affected and interested individuals and organizations opportunities to become informed about, and to express their opinions on, Service actions and policies. In the process, these public views are studied thoroughly and are thoughtfully considered in shaping decisions for refuge management.
public-use sites	Sites identified that are important for public access (including important floatplane and wheeled plane landing areas), camping, hunting, fishing, or other recreational or public uses.
public-use management plan (PUMP)	A public-use management plan (also known as a visitor service plan) guides the management of public use on a refuge. Public use encompasses both recreational and subsistence uses and includes hunting, trapping, fishing, guiding, camping, photography, sightseeing, hiking, and wildlife viewing. A PUMP summarizes how the public is involved in developing issues and alternatives and describes the alternatives developed to manage public use.
purposes of the refuge	The purposes specified in or derived from the law, proclamation, executive order, agreement, public land order, donation document, or administrative memorandum establishing, authorizing, or expanding a refuge, refuge unit, or refuge subunit (USFWS, 602 FW 1.6).

quality (recreation opportunities and experiences)

Quality is defined as the degree to which recreational opportunities and related experiences meet the objectives for which they are planned and managed. The Service develops visitor services programs in consultation with state fish and wildlife agencies and stakeholder input based on the following criteria:

- Promotes safety of participants, other visitors, and facilities
- Promotes compliance with applicable laws and regulations and responsible behavior
- Minimizes or eliminates conflict with fish and wildlife population or habitat goals or objectives in a plan approved after 1997
- Minimizes or eliminates conflicts with other priority general public-use participants
- Minimizes conflicts with neighboring landowners
- Promotes accessibility and availability to a broad spectrum of American people
- Promotes stewardship and conservation
- Promotes public understanding and increases public appreciation of America's natural resources and our role in managing and protecting those resources
- Provides reliable/reasonable opportunity to experience wildlife
- Uses facilities that are accessible and that blend into the natural setting
- Uses visitor satisfaction to help define and evaluate programs

record of decision (ROD)

A concise public record of a decision prepared by the Federal agency, pursuant to NEPA, that contains a statement of the decision, identification of all alternatives considered, identification of the environmentally preferable alternative, a statement whether all practical means to avoid or minimize environmental harm from the alternative selected have been adopted (and if not, why they were not), and a summary of monitoring and enforcement where applicable for any mitigation (40 CFR 1505.2).

recreational fishing

Taking or attempting to take for personal use, not for sale or barter, any fish by hook and line held in the hand or attached to a pole or rod that is held in the hand or is closely attended.

recreation guide

A commercial operator who accompanies clients on the refuge for photography, sightseeing, or other activities not related to hunting or fishing, for either day or overnight trips.

recreational hunting	Taking or attempting to take for personal use, not for sale or barter, a game animal (as defined by the regulatory agency) by any means allowed by the regulatory agency.
recreational fishing or hunting guide	A commercial operator who accompanies recreational fishing or hunting clients on the refuge for day or overnight trips.
Refuge Operating Needs System	The Refuge Operating Needs System (RONS) is a national database that contains a listing of the unfunded operational needs of each refuge. We include projects required to implement approved plans and to meet goals, objectives, and legal mandates.
river classifications	
wild rivers	Those rivers or sections of rivers that are free of impoundments and generally inaccessible except by trail, with watersheds or shorelines essentially primitive and waters unpolluted. These represent vestiges of primitive America.
scenic rivers	Those rivers or sections of rivers that are free of impoundments, with shorelines or watersheds still largely primitive and shorelines largely undeveloped, but accessible in places by roads.
recreational rivers	Those rivers or sections of rivers that are readily accessible by road or railroad, that may have some development along their shorelines, and that may have undergone some impoundment or diversion in the past.
special use permit	A U.S. Fish and Wildlife Service authorization required for all commercial uses of refuge lands and waters. Permits for Alaska Peninsula and Becharof National Wildlife Refuges are issued by the Refuges office in King Salmon.
spike camp	A temporary camp set up by a guide or outfitter to provide overnight accommodations away from base camp (see primitive tent camp).
sport fishing or hunting	See "recreational fishing" or "recreational hunting."
step-down management plan	A plan that provides specific guidance on management subjects (e.g., habitat, public use, fire, safety) or groups of related subjects. It describes strategies and implementation schedules for meeting comprehensive conservation plan goals and objectives.

subsistence uses	The customary and traditional uses by rural Alaska residents of wild, renewable resources for direct personal or family consumption as food, shelter, fuel, clothing, tools, or transportation; for the making and selling of handicraft articles out of nonedible byproducts of fish and wildlife resources taken for personal or family consumption; for barter or sharing for personal or family consumption; and for customary trade (from Section 803 of the Alaska National Interest Lands Conservation Act).
temporary base camp	Serves as a center of operations and overnight accommodations for guests and guides. A temporary base camp usually remains in place for the full season of use (90 to 120 days) but may be removed within 48 hours. It generally consists of larger tents than do primitive camps and often has tent platforms or other rigid floors. A typical camp would include several large guest tents, a cook tent, and a few smaller tents for staff use, showers, waste disposal, storage, etc. In some cases, smaller camps that include only four or five tents and related facilities are used by clients for overnight visits of two to four days. The primary distinction between temporary base camps and primitive camps is the period of occupancy. The specific details of a temporary base camp located on refuge lands would be spelled out in the state land-use permit or refuge special-use permit.
use day	A period of one calendar day (24 hours), or portion thereof, for each entity using a resource. When employed as a measure of human us, it is called a visitor or visitor-use day.
visitor contact station	A staffed or unstaffed facility where the public can learn about the refuge and its resources.
vision statement	A concise statement of the desired future condition of the planning unit, based primarily on the System mission, specific refuge purposes, and other relevant mandates (USFWS, 602 FW 1.6).
visitor day	See "use day."
wilderness	An area essentially undisturbed by human activity, together with its naturally developed life community.

Wilderness	A designated Wilderness, in contrast with those areas where man and his own works dominate the landscape, is hereby recognized as an area where the earth and its community of life are untrammeled by man, where man himself is a visitor who does not remain. A Wilderness area is further defined to mean, in this plan, an area of undeveloped federal land retaining its primeval character and influence, without permanent improvements or human habitation, which is protected and managed to preserve its natural conditions and which (1) generally appears to have been affected primarily by the forces of nature, with the imprint of man's work substantially unnoticeable; (2) has outstanding opportunities for solitude or a primitive and unconfined type of recreation; (3) has at least 5,000 acres of land or is of sufficient size as to make practicable its preservation and use in an unimpaired conditions; and (4) may also contain ecological, geological, or other features of scientific, educational, scenic, or historical value (Wilderness Act 1964).
Wilderness Area	An area designated by the United States Congress to be managed as part of the National Wilderness Preservation System (USFWS, 602 FW 1.6).
wilderness review	The process we use to determine if we should recommend Refuge System lands and waters to Congress for Wilderness designation.
wildlife-dependent recreation	A use of a refuge involving hunting, fishing, wildlife observation and photography, or environmental education and interpretation. These are the six priority public uses of the Refuge System, as established in the National Wildlife Refuge System Administration Act, as amended. Wildlife-dependent recreational uses, other than the six priority public uses, are those that depend on the presence of wildlife.

References Cited

USFWS. "Service Manual." Accessed June 4, 2003. At http://policy.fws.gov/manual.html on the World Wide Web, produced by U.S. Fish and Wildlife Service.

USFWS. 1992. "Cultural Resources Handbook." Accessed June 4, 2003, 2003. At http://www.policy.fws.gov/614fw1.html on the World Wide Web, produced by U.S. Fish & Wildlife Service.

USFWS. 2003. "Annual Report of Lands Under Control of the U.S. Fish and Wildlife Service (as of September 30, 2002)." Accessed June 20, 2003. At http://realty.fws.gov/PDF_Files/AROL2003.pdf on the World Wide Web, produced by U.S. Fish and Wildlife Service, Division of Realty. (PDF file)